SEAS AND OCEANS

Clint Twist

DILLON PRESS
NEW YORK

First American publication 1991 by Dillon Press, Macmillan Publishing Company, 866 Third Avenue, New York, NY 10022

Macmillan Publishing Company is part of the Maxwell Communication Group of Companies

First published by Evans Brothers Limited, 2A Portman Mansions, Chiltern Street, London W1M 1LE.

Typeset by Fleetlines Typesetters, Southend-on-Sea
Printed in Spain by GRAFO, S.A. – Bilbao

Library of Congress Cataloging-in-Publication Data

Twist, Clint.
Seas and oceans / Clint Twist.
p. cm. – (Ecology Watch)
Includes index.
Summary: Examines the diverse life forms found in the world's oceans and the threats they face.
ISBN 0-87518-491-X
1. Ocean – Juvenile literature. [1. Marine biology. 2. Ocean]
I. Title. II. Series.
GC21.5.T88 1991
333.95'2—dc20 91–18086

Acknowledgments

Editor: Su Swallow
Design: Neil Sayer
Production: Jenny Mulvanny

Illustrations: David Gardner, Graeme Chambers
Maps: Hardlines, Charlbury

For permission to reproduce copyright material the author and publishers gratefully acknowledge the following:

Cover Kim Westerskov, Oxford Scientific Films
Title page Jeff Foott, Survival Anglia

p4 Kim Westerskov, Oxford Scientific Films **p5** Jeff Foott, Survival Anglia **p6** (top) Heather Angel, (bottom) Kim Westerskov, Oxford Scientific Films **p8** D. P. Wilson, Eric and David Hosking **p9** Annie Price, Survival Anglia **p10** Norman Myers, Bruce Coleman Limited **p12** Christian Petron, Planet Earth Pictures **p13** Walter Rawlings, Robert Harding Picture Library **p14** Wilkinson/ECOSCENE **p15** Peter Parks, Oxford Scientific Films **p16** Brian Hawkes, Robert Harding Picture Library **p17** (left) K. Ammann, Planet Earth Pictures, (right) Bill Wood, Bruce Coleman Limited **p18** François Gohier, Ardea London Ltd **p19** Dr Gene Feldman, NASA GSFC/Science Photo Library **p21** Nigel Merrett, Planet Earth Pictures **p22** (top) Doug Allan, Oxford Scientific Films, (bottom) B. and C. Alexander, Bruce Coleman Limited **p23** Silvestris/Frank Lane Picture Agency **p24** Robert Pitman, Frank Lane Picture Agency **p25** Robert Harding Picture Library **p26** (left) Lewis Trusty, Oxford Scientific Films, (right) Carl Roessler, Planet Earth Pictures **p27** Peter Scoones, Planet Earth Pictures **p28** Martin Coleman, Planet Earth Pictures **p29** Herwarth Voigtmann, Planet Earth Pictures **p30** (left, top right and bottom right) Annie Price, Survival Anglia, (center right) Soames Summerhays/Biofotos **p31** Jeff Foott, Survival Anglia **p32** (top) Vallee/ECOSCENE, (inset) John Mackinnon, Bruce Coleman Limited, (bottom) Peter Parks, Oxford Scientific Films **p33** Bill Wood, Bruce Coleman Limited **p34** Ian Harwood/ECOSCENE **p35** Bruce Coleman Limited **p37** David Cayless, Oxford Scientific Films **p38** Gerald Cubitt, Bruce Coleman Limited, (inset) Norman Myers, Bruce Coleman Limited **p39** Jon and Des Bartlett, Bruce Coleman Limited **p40** (left) Roger Tidman, Frank Lane Picture Agency, (right) François Gohier, Ardea London Ltd **p41** Jeff Foott, Bruce Coleman Limited **p43** Kurt Amslerr, Planet Earth Pictures **p44** Robert Hessler, Planet Earth Pictures

Contents

Introduction

The salt water of the seas and oceans, which covers more than two-thirds of our planet, provides an environment for all kinds of plants and animals. About 90 percent of **marine** life is concentrated in the shallow waters above the continental shelf, an underwater ledge that runs along many coastlines (see map on page 5). In contrast, the huge ocean plain that makes up most of the ocean bed is like a desert, with few plants or animals living there.

Life in the seas and oceans is divided into a number of **ecosystems**. Different groups of plants and animals live in different water temperatures and at different depths. All these marine ecosystems are now under threat from human activities. Fishing, agriculture, industry, tourism, and even litter are putting the marine environment and its inhabitants under pressure.

For hundreds of years we have behaved as though the seas were limitless, capable of producing an endless supply of fish and capable of absorbing an endless supply of trash. We now know that this is not the case. We know, for example, that **overfishing** is responsible for the decline of many species of fish. As the world's human population increases, so does the demand for seafood. **Mariculture**, or sea farming, may eventually provide us with food without endangering the sea's health, but we have

▽ Untreated sewage is pumped into the sea off many coasts round the world. Here, raw sewage stains the sea off Wellington, New Zealand, close to a surfing beach.

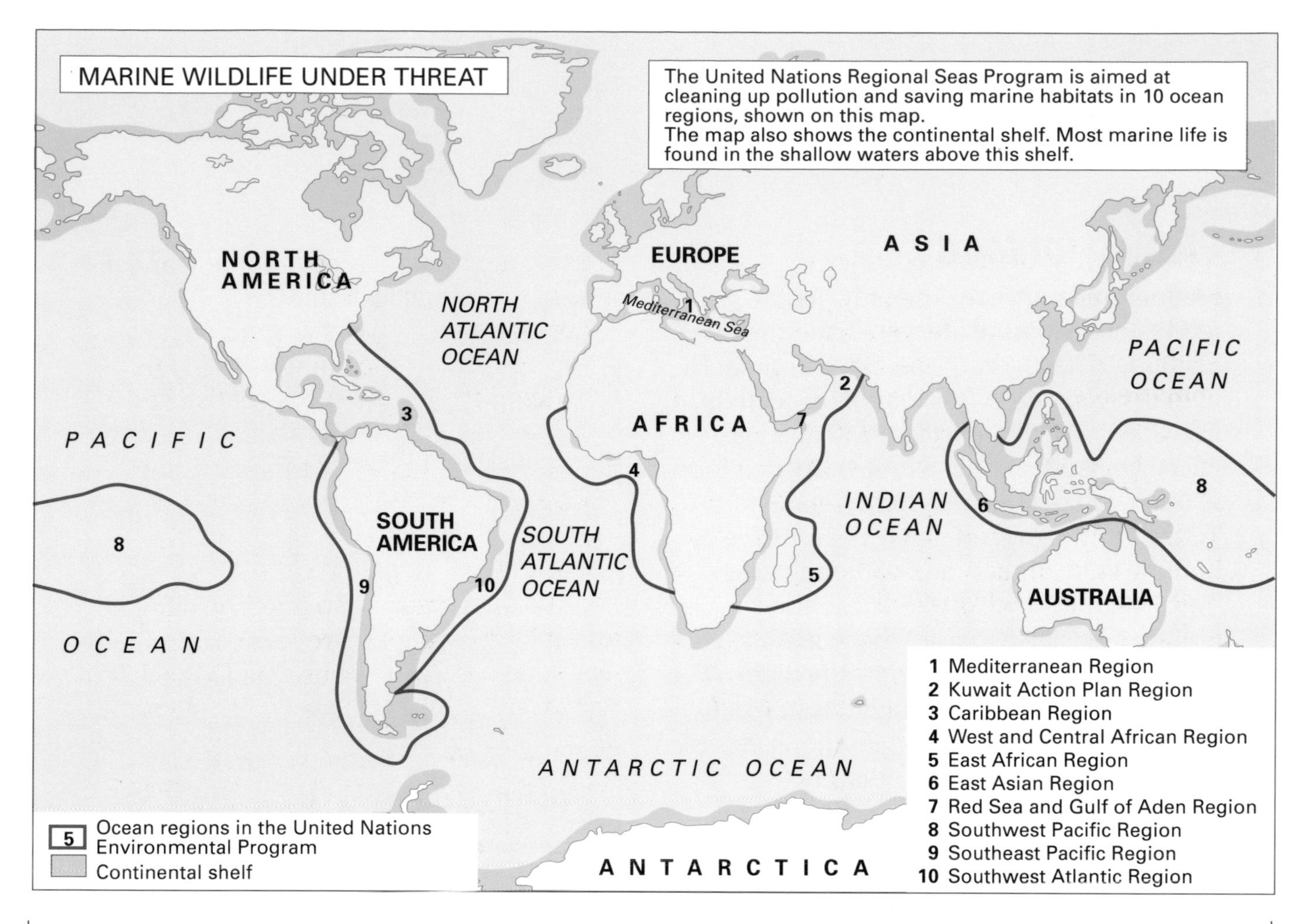

not yet learned how to farm the sea efficiently and without affecting the marine ecosystems.

Some marine species are under threat from **pollution**. Steps have been taken to reduce the amount of pollution in the sea. The dumping of some highly dangerous wastes, such as poison gas and radioactive material, is now largely controlled by international agreement. Oil tankers are now banned from cleaning their tanks at sea, a practice which polluted tens of millions of gallons of seawater at a time. But coastal waters are still being polluted with billions of tons of human, industrial, and agricultural wastes, just in the place where the sea is rich in marine life.

When, in the 1970s, people realized that the seas and oceans were under threat, some groups began to act to save them. In 1975, for example, the United Nations sponsored the Mediterranean Action Plan, which was aimed at cleaning up the world's most polluted sea. This plan has blossomed into the Regional Seas Program, which covers 10 different marine areas. Such schemes are helping the seas and oceans to survive, but more action is needed worldwide if the marine environment is to stay healthy. The future of the seas and oceans lies in our hands.

Words printed in **bold** are explained at the end of each section.

marine—found in, or relating to the sea.
ecosystem—a group of plants and animals which share the same environment.
overfishing—removing wild fish (or other marine animals) faster than they can reproduce themselves, thus causing their numbers to fall.
mariculture—cultivating seafood, rather than collecting it from the wild.
pollution—the contamination of an environment by any substance that is not naturally present.

Life in the sea

Fishing for food

For hundreds of years, the only people interested in marine life were fishermen. Fishermen have a very one-sided approach to their occupation. Their main concern is to find and catch the most fish with the least effort. On land, people who obtain their food in this way are known as hunter-gatherers. Today, only a few isolated tribes still live by hunting wild animals and gathering wild fruit. Their life-style is often described as primitive because most of the world's population obtains its food by the more advanced methods of farming. At sea, our methods have not changed for thousands of years; we are still hunter-gatherers.

Recent developments in science and technology have enabled fishermen to become very efficient hunter-gatherers. Shoals of fish are located by underwater echo sounders, and are then encircled by seine nets (see **Caught in the net**) up to two miles long. The catch is often processed and frozen by factory ships that remain at sea for months at a time until they are fully laden. The problem with all this superefficiency is that the present catch of 90 million tons of fish per year is probably too high to be sustained.

△ A purse seine net is hauled aboard a trawler, off the coast of British Columbia, Canada.

◁ Fishermen on a New Zealand trawler put orange roughy into a container with ice to keep them fresh.

Falling numbers

In many parts of the world, catches of certain fish species have already declined rapidly. During the 1960s, the catch of haddock in the northwest Atlantic dropped by over 90 percent. During the 1970s, the catch of anchovies off the coast of Peru dropped from 13 million tons to less than 2 million tons. In European waters, the herring was once caught in great numbers, but this species has now almost completely disappeared.

Overfishing is only one reason for this fall in numbers. In some cases, the fall of a fish population may be a perfectly natural event. The fall in the Peruvian anchovy catch has been blamed partly on changes in the direction of an ocean current flowing from the middle of the Pacific Ocean. In many cases, it is impossible to say exactly who or what is responsible, ourselves or nature.

One thing is certain, however: Fishing has made the human race an important part of the **ecology** of the seas and oceans. The annual harvest from the sea is about 100 million tons of food. Ninety percent of the food is fish. The remaining 10 percent is made up of invertebrates (animals without a backbone). But most of the animals that live in the sea are in fact invertebrates, not fish. By taking the fish, we are taking the cream of the ocean's crop, on which other marine species depend for food. Some of these species are now threatened with extinction (see page 11).

Caught in the net

Food fish can be divided into two sorts, depending on where they are found.

Pelagic fish, such as mackerel and herring, swim in shoals near the surface. Pelagic fish are usually caught by encircling a shoal with a large net known as a seine.

Demersal fish, such as plaice and sole, swim along the seabed and are often called flatfish because of their shape. Demersal fish are usually scraped off the seabed with a net known as a trawl.

In both cases, the fishermen cannot tell how good a catch is until it has been hauled aboard. If the fish are the wrong species, or are too small, it is by then too late to throw them back. Fishing is often a very wasteful business.

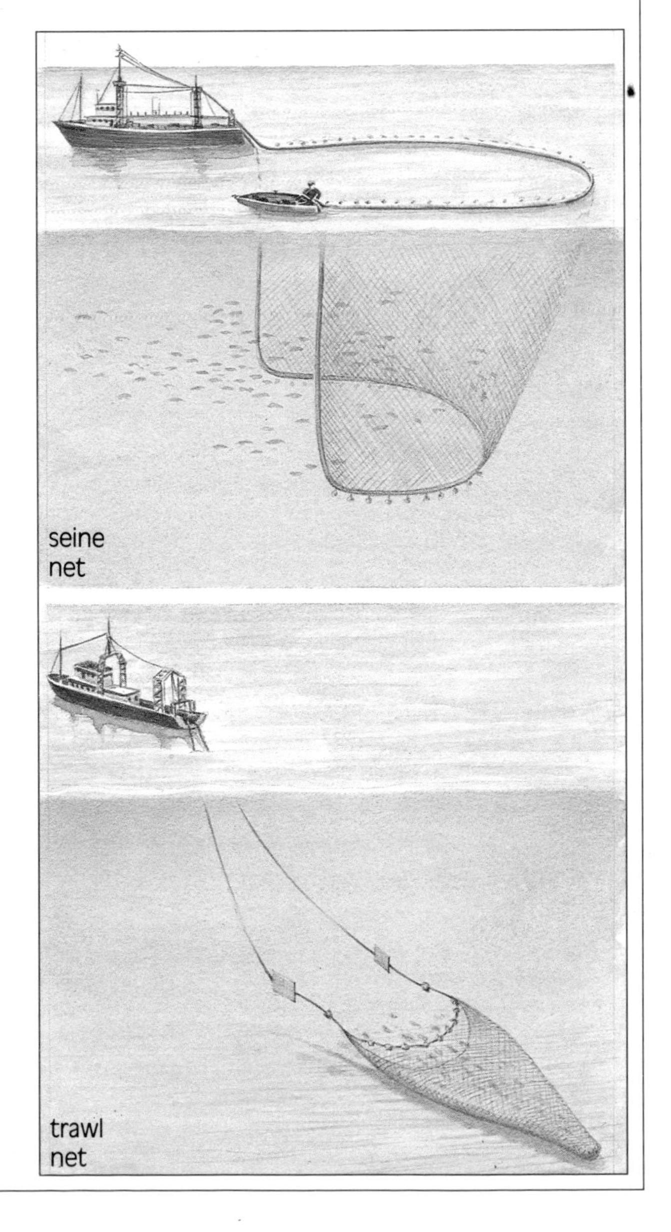

▷ A seine net hangs from floats, and is weighted down at the bottom. When a shoal of fish is trapped, the net is closed at the bottom by pulling on a line. The bag-shaped trawl net is pulled along at a deep level to catch fish in its path.

Good enough to eat?

Not all the fish that are caught are eaten by people. As the numbers of traditional food fish (such as herring and haddock) have fallen, fishermen have turned to other species in order to maintain the size of their catch. In the United States, over 30 percent of the total catch is made up of Atlantic menhaden. But nobody has ever seen this fish on sale. The entire catch of menhaden is ground up and used for animal feed.

Large numbers of other edible fish, such as the sardine caught off West Africa, are also used for animal feed because they are too small to be packaged commercially.

Many people now believe that feeding fish to animals is an extremely wasteful use of the sea's valuable food resources.

A food engine

In the sea, as on land, the plants are the key to all other life forms. In the sea, the most important plants are the smallest. Microscopic phytoplankton drifts near the surface of water, in the top 30 feet of the sea, where plenty of sunlight is available for **photosynthesis**. Indeed, about 70 percent of all photosynthesis that takes place on earth is carried out by these tiny plants. Seawater that contains plenty of phytoplankton looks murky green; the deep blue water that often appears on color photographs may mean that the sea contains little life.

Large numbers of tiny animals known as zooplankton graze on the phytoplankton. Some of these animals spend their whole lives as zooplankton, but many are the larvae, or young, of shellfish and other invertebrates that spend most of their lives on the sea bed. Other zooplankton grow into free-swimming organisms such as sea urchins, jellyfish, and some species of fish.

Links in the food chain

The first and most important link in the ocean's food chain is between the two types of plankton. The plant-eating zooplankton provide food for a wide range of meat-eating invertebrates and small fish. These in turn are eaten by larger animals (mainly fish), until the food chain ends with a top **predator**, such as a shark. Nearly all this activity takes place within 600 feet of the surface. Below these depths, the water is too cold and dark to make an attractive environment for animals that can swim.

Life in the upper level of the seas and oceans provides a constant rain of dead plants and animals that sinks down to the seabed, where it supports a host of animals. Most of the animals that live here are invertebrates. Some, such as crabs, are **scavengers** and are constantly on the move in search of food; others, such as the marine worms, burrow into the seabed and filter food particles from the water. Predators on the seabed include starfish and many species of shellfish. Any food that is not

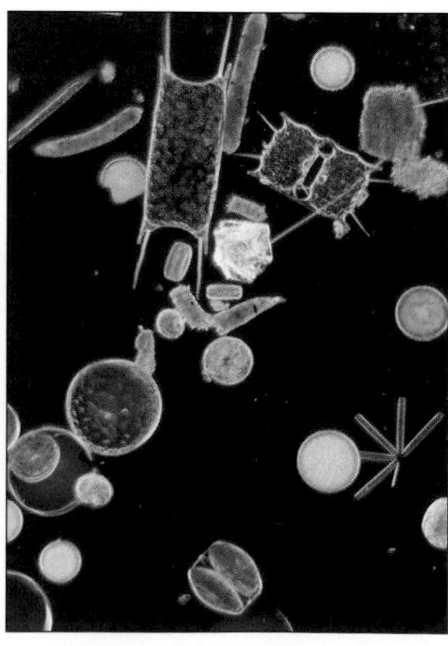

▷ Rockhopper penguins on the Falkland Islands, like other animals in the Antarctic, are at risk from pollution in the sea.

◁ Plankton is made up of phytoplankton (tiny plants, left) and zooplankton (tiny animals, far left).

eaten is broken down by **bacteria** and the **nutrients** are released back into the sea.

In the shallow waters over the continental shelf, free-swimming life and the bottom dwellers share the same water space. Where the water is less than 300 feet deep, the larger seaweeds can find a surface on which to grow. In waters less than 60 feet deep, green seaweed often forms large undersea "meadows." It is this rich supply of plant life that makes fish and other marine animals so plentiful in coastal waters. Any pollution in the water can quickly spread along food chains.

From plankton to penguin

Some forms of pollution increase as they move along a food chain. Substances can build up as one animal eats another, and thus may reach dangerous levels. This kind of buildup is called bioconcentration. One of the first chemicals to cause problems through bioconcentration was the insecticide DDT, which is now banned in many countries. Traces of DDT have been found in the Antarctic Ocean. The levels of DDT in Antarctic predators, such as seals and penguins, are many times greater than in plankton, at the bottom of the food chain.

Life at the top

Within an ecosystem, the various food chains link together to form a single food web. The sun's energy, absorbed by the plants through photosynthesis, is passed around the food web as one animal eats another. However, most of the energy is lost at each feeding stage, and on average only 10 percent of the energy is transferred efficiently. This means that two pounds of fish represents about one ton of plants. It also means that animals that are lower down the food web occur in much greater numbers than those higher up. So life in the sea, as on land, can be arranged into pyramids of feeding.

One ton (2,200 lb) of phytoplankton provides food for 220 lb of zooplankton, which provide food for 22 lb of small fish (such as herring), which provide food for 2 lb of mackerel, which makes a hearty meal for one human being.

The state of the sea

How healthy is the sea? The answer depends on where you look and what you are looking for. A single bucket of seawater will only tell you part of the story, and samples from thousands of different places are needed in order to draw a more complete picture. A true picture of the state of the seas requires a global approach.

Pollution report

In 1990, the United Nations Environmental Program published a report based on scientific studies from all over the world. It contained both good news and bad news. First, the good news:

—Most of the marine environment is still unpolluted.

—None of the polluted areas have so far been damaged beyond repair, and given time should all recover.

—Pollution control does work. In several heavily polluted areas where controls have been introduced, levels of pollution have already started to decline.

However, the UNEP also found some serious problems:

—Our increasing use of the coastline for

◁ When beaches such as this one in Rio de Janeiro, Brazil, are developed for tourists, marine life suffers.

housing, tourism and industry is destroying marine life habitats.
—Beaches are being contaminated by oil and sewage.
—Plastic debris is killing marine animals. Every year hundreds of thousands of marine animals choke on plastic bags or bottles that they have eaten by mistake.

Dying out?

The report also noted that a number of marine animals were in danger of extinction. Most of the marine animals that are currently endangered (some species of seals, whales, dolphins, seabirds, and turtles) come from the top of the food web. There are two reasons for this. First, predators in general, and top predators in particular, have fairly small populations to begin with, because of the pyramid of numbers (see page 10). Second, as predators, they are the first to feel the effects of overfishing by humans. If we take too many fish, the predators do not have enough prey to feed on.

Extinction is a natural process: It is part of the slowest rhythm of life—evolution. But it is very important that it is nature, not human beings, that decides when a particular species becomes extinct.

The science of ecology teaches us that life on our planet exists as an extremely complex balance among *all* the different species that share the global environment. The extinction of even a single species can upset this delicate balance, and there may be a chain of unexpected consequences affecting other species. At present we do not know enough about our planet to work out all the possible consequences. Therefore, whenever we are presented with a choice—to preserve or to allow extinction—it is vital that we respect the whole of our environment and choose to preserve rather than to destroy.

A note on numbers

Counting wild animals is not easy, particularly in the sea, and population figures are always an estimate and sometimes just a guess. Nor do numbers tell the whole story. The degree to which a species is endangered also depends on its geographical range, and on how quickly its population is falling.

As a general rule of thumb, a species with a total population of less than 500 is unlikely to survive in the wild. Group size can also be important. A group of 50 or less is unlikely to survive for long because the death of a single adult represents a 10 percent decline in the breeding population.

Steller's sea cow

In 1741, the explorers who discovered the Bering Strait between Alaska and Siberia also discovered a giant sea cow. This animal was a close relative of the dugongs that live in the Indian Ocean today, but grew to over 26 feet in length. Steller's sea cow (named after one of the explorers) was a big hit with the fur trappers, and thousands were slaughtered every year. Less than 30 years after it had been discovered, Steller's sea cow was hunted into extinction.

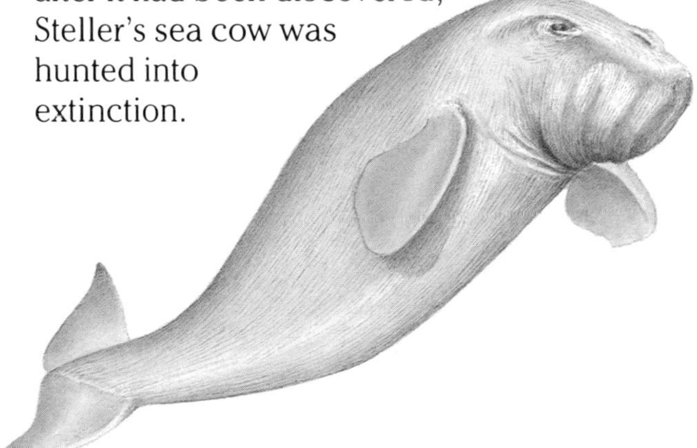

ecology—the relationships among living organisms and their environment.
photosynthesis—the process by which plants use the sun's energy to produce sugars from water and carbon dioxide.
predator—any animal that hunts and eats other animals.
scavenger—any animal that feeds on dead animals.
bacteria—a large group of microscopic organisms.
nutrients—chemicals absorbed by plants for nourishment.

Close-up on the Mediterranean

A polluted sea

In the 1970s, the Mediterranean Sea made headlines as the most polluted area of salt water in the world. Many scientists predicted that by the year 2000 it would become a lifeless environment. We now know that this will not happen, but it is easy to see why the scientists were so concerned.

The Mediterranean is a small sea that is almost entirely surrounded by land. The only outlet to the Atlantic Ocean is through the narrow Straits of Gibraltar (less than 12 miles wide). As a result, there is very little mixing of waters between the Atlantic Ocean and the Mediterranean. Any garbage or waste that is dumped into the Mediterranean tends to stay there for a long time. Pollution therefore builds up much faster than elsewhere.

Unfit for swimming

During the mid-1970s some 400 million tons of waste was pumped into the sea every year. Most of the sewage from 120 coastal cities was flushed straight into the sea without any form of treatment. So it is hardly surprising that by the late 1970s, one quarter of all the beaches in the Mediterranean were considered unfit for swimming because of the dangers to human health from untreated sewage.

Unfit for eating

Even more upsetting were the effects on marine life from other forms of pollution.

▽ The blue water of the Mediterranean off the coast of France looks clean, but is it?

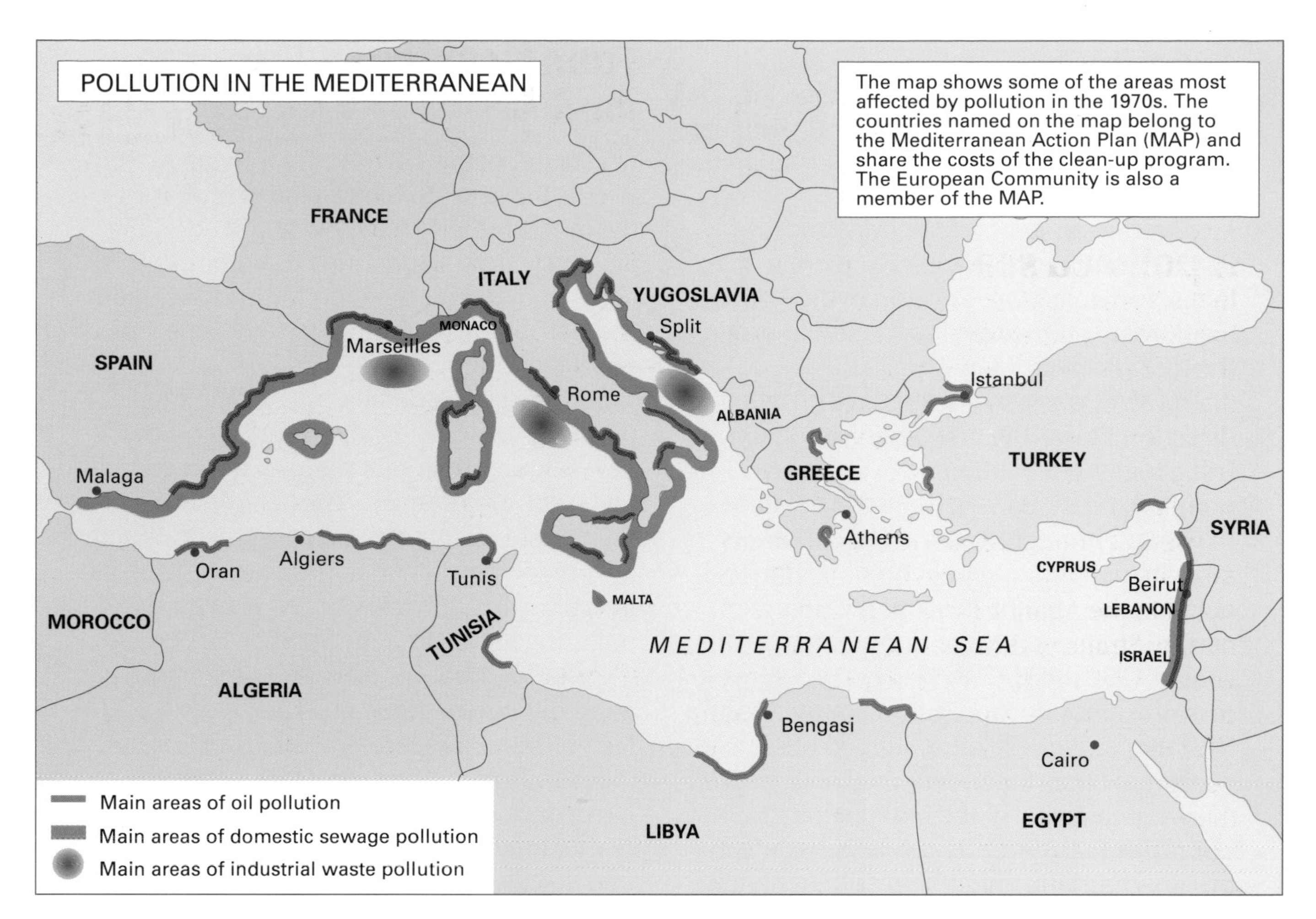

Waste products from industry and chemical sprays from farming wash into rivers and end up in the sea. **Tuna** caught in the Mediterranean were found to contain three times as much mercury as tuna from the Atlantic. Mercury is highly poisonous and the amounts found in Mediterranean tuna meant that they were not fit for people to eat. Over 90 percent of the edible shellfish that were collected in some areas also had to be rejected because they contained poisonous levels of pesticide.

When this information was made public, people became very worried. Many people who live around the Mediterranean make their living from the sea, and fishermen were not the only ones facing a grim future. Some of the poorer Mediterranean countries rely upon the income from tourism to keep their national economy going. If the sea became a filthy and lifeless environment, who would want to spend a holiday there?

▷ Tuna that has been frozen on board is unloaded from a French ship.

A plan of action

In 1975, the United Nations arranged for representatives from 17 of the Mediterranean countries to meet and discuss the situation. As a result of that meeting, the Mediterranean Action Plan (MAP) was created. Although it is called a plan, it is in fact an organization. The aim of the MAP is to prevent and fight pollution, and to protect the marine environment.

The MAP was a major step in the right direction. It was the first organization to bring together countries with different political, religious, and economic statuses to work to protect the environment. It was also the first international organization to achieve real results. In 1976, the member countries agreed to stop dumping waste at sea. In 1980 the MAP agreed on measures to limit the amount of pollution coming from the land; and in 1982 they agreed to set aside protected areas for endangered species.

The great value of the MAP is that the countries that surround the Mediterranean are now working together for a better future for their sea. It is not yet possible to say that the Mediterranean is cleaner than it was in 1975. But it is certainly a lot cleaner than it would have been without the MAP.

From factories and farms to the sea

One result of the 1975 Mediterranean Action Plan is that the Mediterranean is probably the most studied area of water in the world. Scientists from 83 marine laboratories situated in the member countries have spent the last 15 years examining every aspect of marine pollution.

Sewage is one of the easier pollution problems to solve. Under the MAP, many new sewage treatment plants have been built and more are planned. These have an immediate effect on the environment. When the French city of Marseilles started using its new plant in 1987, overall levels of marine pollution in the area dropped by 75 percent.

Pollution from industry and agriculture is more difficult to clean up. The Mediterranean receives waste from thousands of factories and farms that lie close to its shores, and from many more farther inland. Each year the rivers that run into the sea carry hundreds of thousands of tons of chemical pollutants from agriculture

▽ Waste metals from factories pour into this pit, which empties into the Mediterranean.

and industry. Many of these chemicals are deadly poisons, and all of them are harmful to the marine environment.

Some of the most dangerous chemicals are those known as **PCBs**. These are used in the manufacture of plastics and electrical equipment. Large quantities from old machinery dumped in the sea will slowly leak out into the water. In order to study the effect of pollution from PCBs, the MAP decided to keep a careful check on one **organism**. PCBs build up in the tissue of certain animals, particularly shellfish, so the Mediterranean mussel was chosen as the indicator species. In some places, these mussels now contain 300,000 times more PCBs than the surrounding seawater. Even this amount is not enough to threaten the mussel—yet. But in the long run, both marine and human life will be affected if pollution continues to poison the sea.

Unlike industry, agriculture dumps very little pollution deliberately. Farmers would like their fertilizers and pesticides to stay on the land where they are sprayed. But every year, the rain washes huge quantities into the rivers, and so into the sea. Some of the ingredients of chemical pesticides (dioxins, for example) are the same as those in nerve gas, and are designed to be deadly in very small quantities. Only about 90 tons of these substances enter the Mediterranean each year, but like some metals and PCBs, they can build up in the tissues of certain marine animals.

A much more immediate threat comes from the nitrates and phosphates in fertilizers. These substances provide nutrients for growing crops. When they reach the sea, they feed the microscopic **algae** drifting in the water. Where these nutrients build up (often near the mouth of rivers) they cause **eutrophication**. The algae "bloom"—they grow and multiply many times faster than normal—until the surface of the sea is covered with a thick floating mat of algae. When the nutrients are used up, the algae die very quickly and start to decompose. The process of decomposition removes oxygen from the water. Without oxygen, other marine life suffocates. Algal blooms can develop from natural causes, but the marine life quickly recovers. If pollution is the cause, the effects can be much more serious.

▽ Other marine life may suffer when this plankton bloom, over the Great Barrier Reef, Australia, dies.

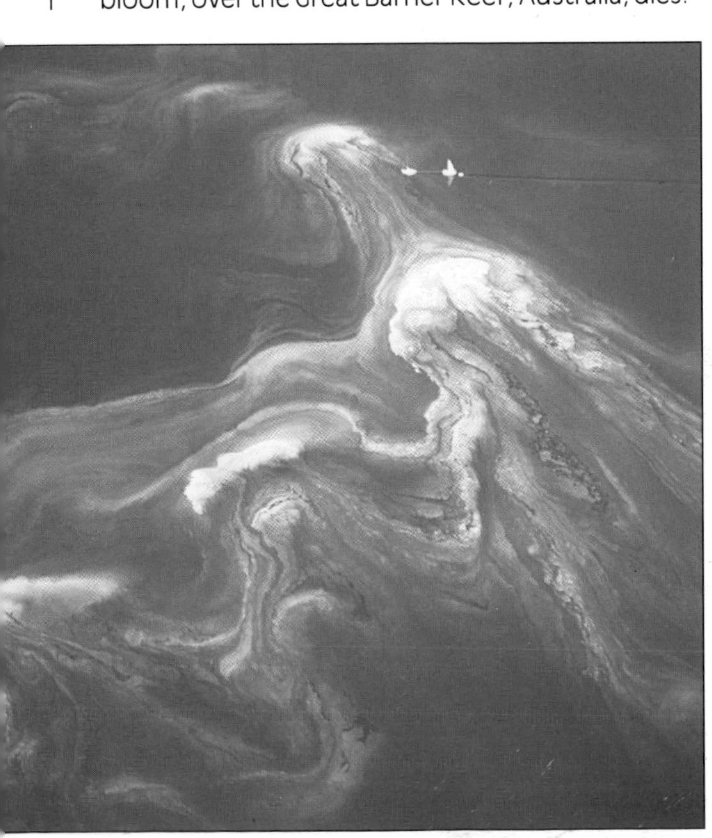

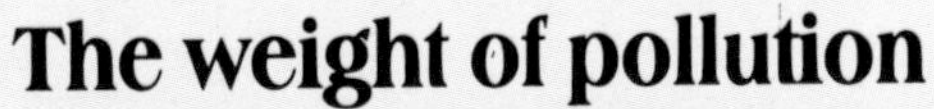

The weight of pollution

Despite the considerable achievements of the MAP to date, pollution continues to pour into the Mediterranean. A recent progress report lists the following annual totals of waste products from industry and agriculture:

	tons
Mineral oils	120,000
Phenols	12,000
Detergents	60,000
Mercury	100
Lead	3,800
Chromium	2,400
Zinc	2,000
Phosphates	320,000
Nitrates	800,000

Endangered species

The Mediterranean is not an especially fertile sea, and fish populations have been declining steadily for some time. Quite apart from pollution, the sea is also suffering the effects of 2,000 years of intensive fishing, and it now produces less than 1 percent of the world's total catch. The Mediterranean contains about 500 different species of fish, 100 of which are found only in this sea. As far as we know, none of the fish species is yet endangered. However, several of the larger animals—mammals, birds, and reptiles—are in very great danger.

The lonely seals

One mammal, the Mediterranean monk seal, stands at the edge of extinction. The monk seal feeds mainly on squid and fish, and the seals have been feeling the effects of the falling numbers of fish. But a shortage of food is only a small part of the story.

Inquisitive and hungry seals have sometimes been seen stealing some of the catch from a fisherman's net. So fishermen see them as thieves and pests, and have

▽ In the Mediterranean, the monk seal is an endangered species.

hunted them for hundreds of years, often clubbing newborn seal pups to death as they rest on a beach. The remaining seals no longer go anywhere near beaches, and some live in caves with underwater entrances. The monk seal is now protected by law in nearly all the Mediterranean countries.

When their numbers were greater, monk seals lived a communal life in herds of up to 50 animals. Today, their descendants lead a very lonely existence, living by themselves, or in groups of two or three. There are still a few seals off Algeria, Bulgaria, Sicily, Sardinia, and possibly Turkey and Greece. The exact location of some groups is kept secret for their own safety.

Reserves have been established for the seals, but they are not always effective. Whenever a monk seal leaves the reserve in search of food, it may be attacked by fishermen. At the beginning of 1988, the Mediterranean monk seal was declared an emergency case.

The plight of the pelican

The pelican is one of Europe's rarest birds. There are only two species, and both are found in the marshy coastlands of the eastern Mediterranean. The white pelican is more numerous, with about 5,000 birds in total. The plight of the Dalmatian pelican is much more precarious. There are only about 500 left, and most of these live on reserves that have been established under the MAP. The reserves are necessary because the pelicans feed on fish, and are sometimes killed by fishermen.

Turtles and tourism

The loggerhead turtle is the only sea turtle that lives in the Mediterranean. In the past, it was hunted nearly out of existence for its juicy flesh. More recently, it has become a victim of tourism. As beaches are developed for vacationers, their breeding grounds are destroyed and the loggerhead turtle is now seriously endangered. Protected areas, such as the one at Dalyan in Turkey, have now become a major part of efforts to save the remaining turtles, and with luck the Mediterranean sea turtles will survive. (See also page 30.)

△ The loggerhead turtle is now protected in parts of the Mediterranean.

◁ White pelican

tuna—the largest and most valuable of the food fish. Some species grow to more than 1,300 lb.
PCBs—polychlorinated biphenyls. A group of very poisonous chemicals used in the manufacture of plastic.
organism—any living plant or animal.
algae—a group of plants that includes phytoplankton and seaweeds.
eutrophication—a process by which algae multiply very rapidly and then die. Rotting algae remove oxygen from the water, suffocating other marine life.

Mammals in the open sea

Whales in the wild

Whales are mammals that have made the ocean their permanent home and have adapted completely to life in the open sea. These gentle giants travel thousands of miles each year, and some species sing to each other across the ocean depths.

Baleen whales

Whales are divided into two groups, baleen whales and toothed whales. The baleen whales include the blue, gray, humpback, bowhead, sei, fin, and minke whales. They feed mainly on zooplankton which they filter out of seawater through bony fringed plates, or baleen, that hang from the upper jaw. A baleen whale feeds by swimming with its mouth open. When the plates are full of food, the whale closes its mouth, wipes the baleen with its tongue, and swallows. A large whale may consume up to three tons of zooplankton per day. Some of the smaller species, such as the minke, often feed on shoals of small fish.

In the tropical oceans, zooplankton are always available because phytoplankton, on which the zooplankton feed, can grow all year round under strong sunlight (see page 19). In polar waters, where it is dark for six months of the year, phytoplankton only grow in summer. Huge midsummer blooms,

▽ The humpback whale leaps out of the water as it feeds on krill on the sea's surface.

especially those in Antarctic waters, are probably the most productive of all marine ecosystems. Each year, many baleen whales make a long migration from their breeding grounds in the warm waters around the equator to the rich feeding grounds of the polar plankton blooms.

How baleen whales feed

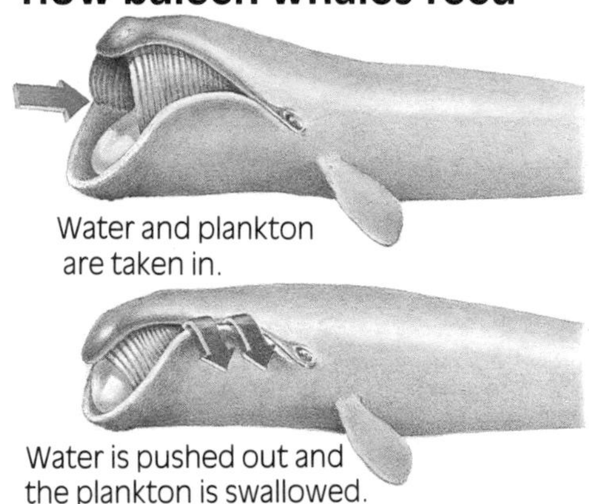

▽ Water rich in phytoplankton looks pink on this satellite picture. (The satellite has not collected information from the areas shown as gray.)

Krill

The waters of a plankton bloom contain zooplankton by the billion. In the waters of the Antarctic, about half of all zooplankton consists of Antarctic krill, a shrimplike animal about 2 in long. Plankton blooms produce as much as 500 million tons of krill each year.

Some countries have already started fishing for krill, although less than a million tons per year is taken at present. It has been suggested that we could harvest much larger quantities of krill: Since we have already killed most of the whales, most of the krill is now going to waste.

Unfortunately, food webs are not that simple. The decrease in whales has been matched by an increase in seals and penguins. Krill that is no longer feeding whales is feeding increased numbers of fish, which in turn are feeding increased numbers of seals and penguins.

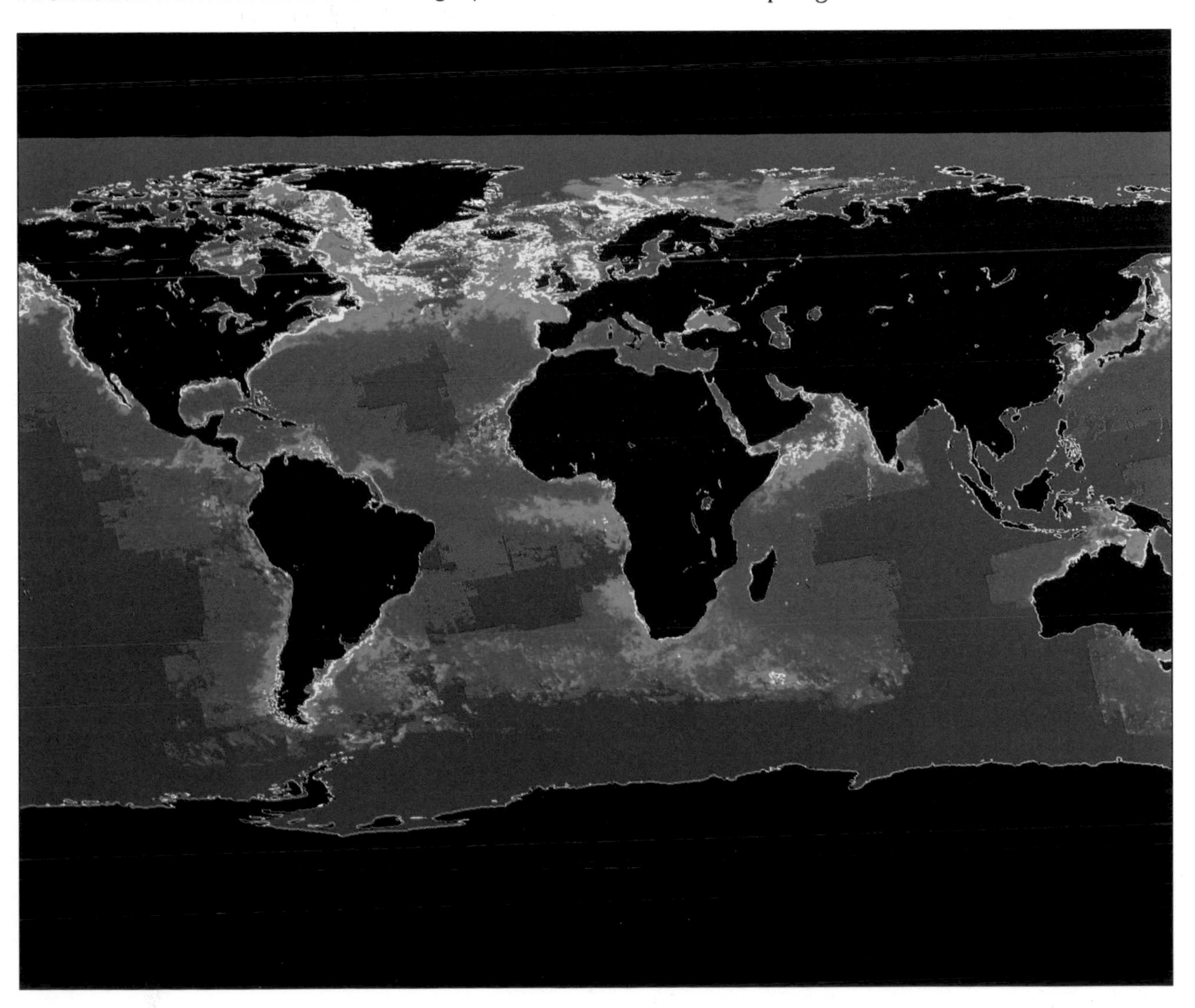

The ecosystem has already adapted to the decline of the whales. If we now start harvesting krill on a large scale, it is bound to cause problems somewhere. Less krill means less fish, which means fewer seals and penguins, and fewer whales. By feeding ourselves, we make other species go hungry.

Toothed whales

The toothed whales include all the other marine mammals that have a fishlike appearance: sperm whales, beaked whales, killer whales, and many species of porpoises and dolphins. They are all predators, and feed mainly on fish and squid. The sperm whale is the largest of the toothed whales, and can weigh up to 70 tons. It is also the deepest diver in the sea. Sperm whales are believed to descend beyond 6500 feet in search of their favorite prey, the giant squid.

The beaked whales are the least known of the whales. They spend most of their time in the depths hunting fish, and some species can remain underwater for up to two hours at a time.

▽ The chart shows the decline in numbers of the large baleen whales during the 20th century, which was due entirely to whaling by humans. When whaling was stopped, the decline in numbers halted, but the populations have so far not increased again.

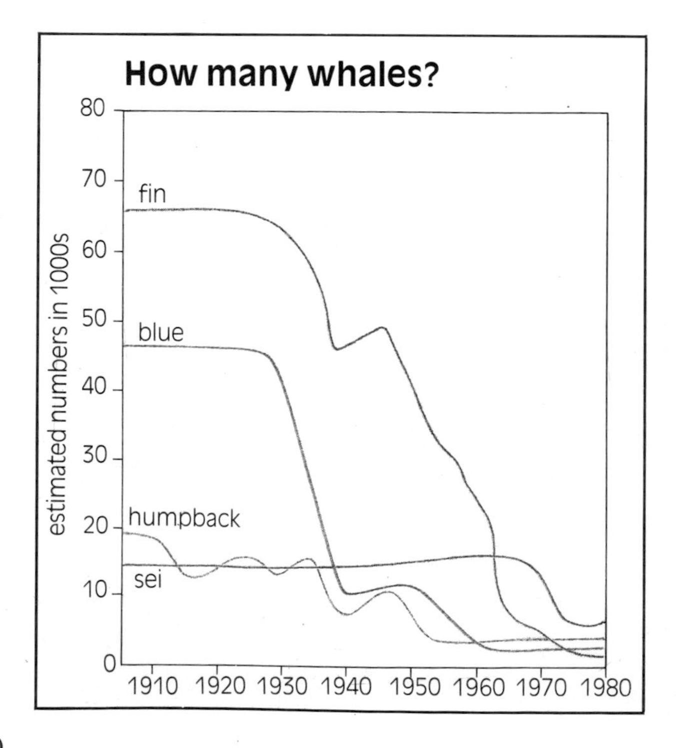

Killer whales are the most ferocious of all marine predators. They swim at the very top of the marine food web but generally leave other mammals alone, content to feed on fish such as salmon. There are no confirmed reports of killer whales killing humans.

Whales under attack

Like other mammals, whales breathe oxygen from the atmosphere. Some speices can remain underwater for long periods of time, but all whales must come to the surface in order to breathe. When they are at the surface, whales become vulnerable to their only natural enemies—humans.

Whaling for profit

During the 20th century, we have been responsible for a disastrous decline in the number of whales. Hundreds of thousands of these huge, harmless creatures have been slaughtered. Some species, including the blue whale, are in danger of extinction. The whales have been killed for their meat and for their blubber. Blubber is a thick layer of fatty tissue below the skin of marine mammals which helps to insulate them against the cold. It can be refined into high-quality oil.

Whaling used to be a major industry. Whaling fleets from many countries set off for months at a time in search of fat targets for their harpoons. Between 1900 and 1950, commercial whalers killed most of the large baleen whales, and when the largest whales became scarce, the whalers turned their attention to smaller and smaller species.

In the 1930s the gray whale had become so scarce that it was declared **commercially extinct**. It has been protected ever since, and some gray whale populations have now grown nearly to their original size. Other species have been less fortunate. The blue whale and the humpback whale were not protected until the 1960s, by which time their populations had fallen to a few thousand of each. Whaling for the smaller species continued into the 1980s.

▷ A sei whale and a fin whale lie on the deck of a whaling ship.

When the fall in numbers became widely known, the sad fate of the whales caused a wave of public concern. Several wildlife and environmental organizations mounted an international campaign called Save the Whales. With the support of hundreds of marine scientists, they eventually persuaded governments, and then the International Whaling Commission (which controls the whaling industry) to take action. Since 1986, all forms of commercial whaling have been banned.

This old harpoon was once used for whaling.

▽ An Inuit (Eskimo) hunter in Greenland has caught a narwhal, a toothed whale which has a long, spiral tusk.

Whaling for food

Subsistence whaling (catching whales to feed one's family, not to sell) is the only form of whaling that is now legal. In remote parts of Alaska, Greenland, and Siberia, some native inhabitants have always depended on whales as a source of food. For this reason, they are permitted to kill a small number of whales each year, which does not pose a threat to the whale population as a whole.

Who is right?

The debate about whaling continues. Some countries feel that whales should be a source of food for all. They argue that we should start whaling again on a limited basis, to establish exactly how many whales can be killed without endangering the population.

Other countries argue that some whales, such as minke whales, are now so numerous that they have become a pest because of the amount of fish that they eat. These countries want to limit the number of whales in order to protect human food supplies. There are no easy answers to the whaling debate, and nobody can be certain exactly how many whales is enough.

Voices from the deep

How do you find a humpback whale when it is underwater? One way is to listen for its song. Some whales make sounds that can be recorded on underwater microphones. Recent research on the humpback whale has shown that these sounds are actually complex songs. A whale song sounds very strange to human ears, a long series of sighs, groans, and squeals. These songs can be detected underwater at distances up to 20 miles.

All the whales in a particular region of ocean share the same basic song, but each whale sings its own version. Humpbacks usually only sing when they are migrating, or during the breeding season. Scientists believe that their songs are mainly a way of saying "Hello, this is who I am," to any other whales that might be nearby. However, there are other aspects of the songs which are less easy to understand. Individual bits of the song are constantly changing, and over a period of about eight years the entire song is completely rewritten. Some scientists have suggested that the songs might also be the whales' own way of recording the history of their group.

Care for the killer whale

Many people believe that trained-animal shows are cruel. In one sense, captivity is an unnatural life-style for any wild animal, especially those used to the open spaces of the ocean. However, there are signs that the goodwill earned by killer whales in captivity is helping to protect others in the wild.

On the coast of Vancouver Island in Canada there is a very special beach where killer whales come to play in the shallow water. Only two other beaches like it are known in the whole world. When a logging company wanted to cut down trees near the beach, marine scientists asked local people to help protect the beach but without much hope of success. Killer whales eat lots of fish, and fishing is an important local industry. However, they got a pleasant surprise. The local people did care about the whales, and together they have persuaded the logging company to keep away and let the whales play in peace.

▷ A killer whale entertains the crowds at a marine park in San Diego.

The smallest whales

Porpoises and dolphins are actually toothed whales, but are usually treated as a separate group. There are more than 30 species, and some, such as the river dolphins, are found only in one particular area. Others, such as the common and bottle-nosed dolphins, are found in all the warmer seas and oceans. Dolphins have a long-standing reputation for being the friendliest of all marine animals. There are many stories of dolphins helping swimmers in distress, and they are often seen swimming alongside a boat, apparently just keeping the crew company.

There are no international restrictions on the hunting of dolphins and porpoises because, until very recently, they were thought to be unnecessary. People seemed willing to repay the dolphins' friendly approaches with respect, and most fishermen left them alone. Unfortunately, this is no longer the case. Since the collapse of the whaling industry, some 20 countries have begun harvesting dolphins and porpoises for food. The number of animals caught each year is still fairly small, but it is increasing steadily.

▷ These dolphins are on sale in a Japanese market. To prevent dolphins being trapped by accident, a new seine net with a rim of fine mesh allows the dolphins to escape (right, below).

▽ Dolphins often swim together in groups. A large group may have several hundred dolphins.

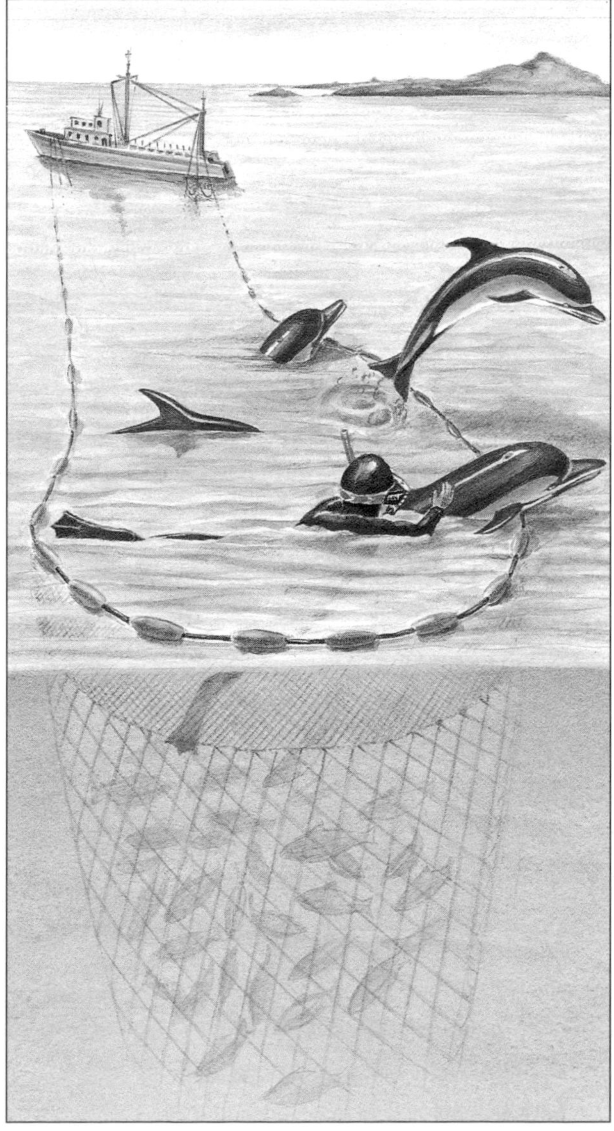

Dolphins are dying

Thousands of dolphins are killed "accidentally." Some become entangled in 12-mile-long gill-nets that are sometimes called "walls of death." Others are trapped by fishermen out for tuna. Dolphins and tuna are often found near each other. The dolphins swim at the surface, where the fishermen can see them, while the tuna remain hidden underwater. It is common fishing practice to enclose a school of dolphins with nets, in the hope of also netting tuna. In the United States, there are now regulations that the nets must be specially adapted so that the dolphins can escape. Some boats even carry divers who get into the water to help the dolphins, but this is quite rare.

Marine scientists estimate that some 500,000 dolphins and porpoises are now being killed each year. They predict that if this rate of killing continues, several species will become extinct by the year 2000.

Some of the most endangered of all mammals are the dolphins that live in the world's great rivers. In China's Yangtze River, the Baiji (whitefin dolphin) now numbers less than 200, and the Indus susu (Indian river dophin) is reduced to around 500 individuals. Its close relative, the Ganges susu, has fared only slightly better, with a population of around 4,000.

At sea, dolphin and porpoise populations are much more difficult to estimate. The Vaquita, which lives only in the Gulf of California, is known to be under threat, and possibly only 10,000 remain. Among the wider-ranging dolphins, the dusky, rough-toothed, spinner, and striped dolphins have all suffered losses from fishermen. These species probably face extinction unless the slaughter is stopped.

commercially extinct—a term applied to any species that was once collected from the wild, but which now exists in numbers too small to make organized collection worthwhile.

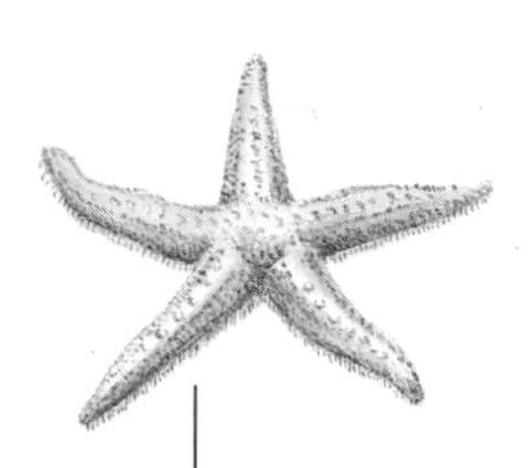

Tropical seas

Coral reefs

A coral reef is the most complex and beautiful of all marine environments. Brightly colored corals grow in many shapes and sizes, creating homes for all kinds of marine life. Coral will not grow in water below 66°F, and reefs (ridges of coral) only occur in **tropical** and **subtropical** regions. Reefs vary greatly in size. Small reefs grow in a bay, while the Australian Great Barrier Reef stretches for more than 1,200 miles. Reefs are extremely fertile ecosystems, and the water around a reef may have hundreds of times more marine life than the surrounding sea. This whole ecosystem is quite literally built by the coral itself.

Usually, corals live in colonies of thousands of individual **polyps**, tiny animals that look like sea anemones. Each species forms colonies in a particular way and has its own shape and color. The coral polyp covers itself with a stony skeleton made from the minerals dissolved in seawater. As corals grow, one generation builds upon the skeletons of its parents, and gradually the individual colonies, and the reefs as a whole, increase in size.

Food, food everywhere

Cemented firmly in place, the polyps feed on plants and animals. They capture zooplankton by waving tentacles which draw the food into the polyp's mouth. Particles of plant material drifting in the water are trapped on the polyp's sticky surface and absorbed. However, the energy that the coral animal receives from feeding is not enough to build reefs. Corals get the rest of the energy they need from the sun.

Thousands of single-celled algae (tiny, simple plants) live inside each polyp. In some cases the algae make up 75 percent of a polyp's weight. The algae carry out photosynthesis in sunlight, and some of the sugar that they produce leaks into the coral animal's body. In ways that are not yet fully understood, the algae also help the polyp to build its stony skeleton. In return, the polyp

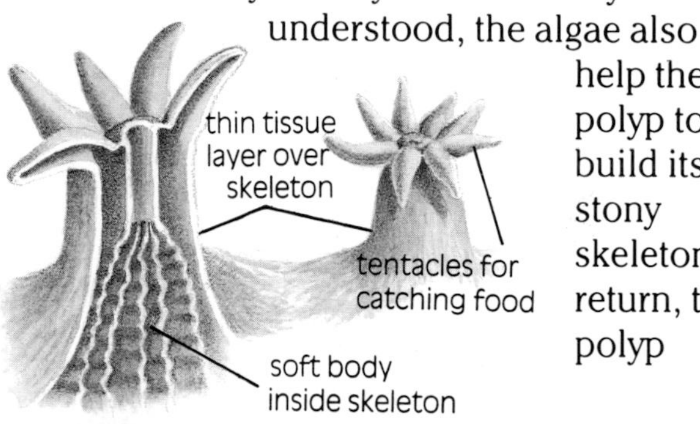

A coral reef is home to groupers (right), clownfish and sea anemones (left), moray eels (below), and many more.

provides the algae with a fairly safe place to live. This type of cooperation between two species is known as **symbiosis**. It is quite rare between large organisms, but is fairly common among microscopic organisms.

Living coral is found only in water less than 300 feet deep, where there is still enough light for the algae to photosynthesize. Most species can only grow well in water less than 200 feet, and the largest corals (up to 6½ feet across) are found only in the shallowest waters. Coral reefs are therefore mainly confined to coastal waters, although they can also grow on the tops of undersea ridges and volcanoes, and may eventually form islands known as atolls.

Living together

Corals provide a three-dimensional environment for many animals that feed directly on the corals or on the seaweeds and sponges that grow among them. The grazers in turn attract predators of all shapes and sizes. The food web of a coral reef is very complex and very efficient.

Life on the reef is a very crowded affair. Among the inhabitants there are many examples of cooperation between species. Tiny fish are protected from the poisonous tentacles of sea anemones and they keep the anemones clean by eating waste food particles. Hermit crabs often share their borrowed shell with a marine worm. The worm is content to feed on the crab's leftovers and may help to keep their shared home clean and neat.

Underwater health service

The reef even has its own health care experts. Some species of fish and shrimp feed on **parasites** that attach themselves to larger fish. These "cleaner" animals gather at certain places on a reef and advertise their services. The fish usually have brightly colored stripes, and the shrimps wave their antennae to attract passing "customers."

These marine body-cleaners are essential to the overall health of the reef. When they were removed in an experiment from one small reef, all the large fish died because they had too many parasites.

Slow growth or a quick death?

Corals grow very slowly, less than half an inch per year, and even small reefs have taken thousands of years to develop. The core of the reef is made of tough limestone rock and can withstand the full force of a storm. But the outer, living layer is extremely fragile and is easily broken. Each year, storms damage corals, but in the long run human activities present a much greater threat.

Mining the reefs

In several parts of the Pacific Ocean, mostly off Sri Lanka and around the island of Bali, huge areas of reef have been removed by mining to provide stone for roads and buildings and lime for making cement. The removal of a reef not only destroys an ecosystem, it also leaves the coastline exposed to the full fury of the sea. The Sri Lankan government has now stopped many reef-mining operations as part of a scheme to protect the marine environment and prevent coastal **erosion**.

△ This beach has been eroded by the sea as coral has been removed to provide lime for building.

The tourist trade

The growth of tourism over the last 30 years has caused other problems. The construction of seafront hotels, harbors, and marinas often involves the destruction of whole sections of a reef. The popularity of sailing and boating in tropical sunlight also causes problems out at sea. Leisure-time sailors tend to see reefs as underwater obstructions to be hacked out of the way, and a carelessly dropped anchor can smash years of growth to splinters in an instant.

The beauty of a coral reef is best seen from underwater. Sadly, underwater tourists are often tempted to take just a small piece as a memento. This activity not only spoils the beauty of the reef, it also kills it very slowly.

Thousands of tons of the most attractive varieties of coral are "harvested" to be sold as souvenirs or carved into ornaments and jewelry. Bit by bit, reefs are disappearing before the eyes of concerned local inhabitants. In some areas, the rare black coral is now almost extinct.

Our enthusiasm for exotic animals is also threatening other tropical species. Many of the most valuable seashells are created by animals that live on the reef. Perfect specimens are not found on the beach, but are obtained by diving for live animals. As many as 99 out of every 100 of these will later be thrown away because their shells are not quite perfect enough.

Fish for the tanks

Millions of wild fish are also taken each year for the international aquarium trade. In 1980, the United States alone imported more than 200 million tropical fish, and many of these were taken from coral reefs. In some Asian countries, professional "fishnappers" use poisons to dope all the fish in the vicinity, and then scoop up only the ones that they want, leaving the others to be eaten by birds.

If the commercial harvesting of exotic species continues, some species of coral, shellfish, and fish are bound to disappear. This will create a series of small holes in the food web and other relationships which bind the coral ecosystem together.

Sight-seeing and science

Coral reefs deserve to be seen by as many people as possible. They represent nature at its very best.

In the Caribbean, where the destructive effects of tourism have been greatest, the Bonaire Marine Park aims to encourage both tourism and research. Two areas have been set aside as reserves where diving is prohibited and the scientists can work. In the rest of the park, underwater sight-seeing is encouraged, and the scientists must put up with a certain amount of accidental damage caused by inexperienced divers. The first 10 years have been encouraging, and the example of Bonaire shows that tourism and conservation can exist side by side.

Creating coral

Many of the airplanes that were shot down over the Pacific during World War II have by now been covered by small reefs. One way to replace reefs destroyed by people is to sink suitable bases that will encourage

△ In warm, tropical waters coral may grow over wrecks of sunken ships and planes.

corals to grow. In some parts of the world, this "seeding" of a reef has already been tried out. Large piles of old tires and abandoned cars have been placed on the seabed. Although they will remain unsightly for many years, they will soon start to accumulate a covering of life and will eventually form the core of a living reef.

Sea turtles

Sea turtles are the largest and most successful marine **reptiles**, and are found throughout the warm seas and oceans. Their populations have been severely reduced by human activity and they are now endangered. There are only six species of marine turtle. The green, loggerhead, hawksbill, flatback, and ridley turtles all have hard shells. The leatherback turtle is the largest species (up to 1,500 pounds) and as its name suggests has a tough, leathery shell.

Some species, especially the green turtle, are very good to eat. Others are highly prized for their shells, which are used to make ornaments and jewelry, or for their skins, which can be made into leather. Sea turtles are easily caught at sea, but they are at their most vulnerable when the females come ashore to lay their eggs on sandy beaches.

Stranded on the beach

Sea turtles spend most of their lives ranging across the oceans, feeding mainly on jellyfish, shellfish, and crabs. They breed only every two to four years, and always return to the beaches where they themselves were born, often traveling more than 600 miles in order to do so. Beaches that are used by large numbers of turtles are known as rookeries and may be shared by more than one species.

Turtles always come out of the sea in the same place and at the same time of year. This makes it easy for people to collect the eggs to eat, and so the numbers of turtles have fallen. Noisy tourists with cameras have

A green turtle (left) comes ashore to lay her eggs (top). When the babies hatch (middle), they make their way back down the beach to the sea (bottom).

also affected turtle populations. If turtles are disturbed, they may not lay any eggs at all. Many governments now protect their turtles before the animals disappear completely.

In the wild, up to half of the newly hatched turtles may be eaten by crabs or birds as they make their way down the beach to the sea. In order to give the turtles a better start in life, some eggs are taken from the sand to be hatched and raised under human supervision before being released safely into the sea.

A new zoo

In Australia, the authorities have combined protection with tourism to create an "open" turtle zoo. Mon Repos beach in Queensland is one of the largest rookeries in the southern Pacific, and is visited by hundreds of turtles each year. The rookery is now protected, but it is also open to the public.

Watching turtles come ashore by moonlight is a thrilling experience, and one that has become a firm favorite with many Australian vacationers. Given the right approach, it *is* possible to please both the turtles and the tourists.

Sea cows

Manatees and dugongs are relatives of the extinct Steller's sea cow (see page 11). Now their own future is far from certain.

Manatees are found in the Atlantic Ocean, along the coasts of South and Central America, and parts of West Africa. Dugongs are found only in the Pacific and Indian oceans. Both species feed only on seaweed. When they are not feeding, manatees spend most of their time resting on the bottom. Dugongs prefer to bask in sunlight at the surface. The animals are gentle and slow-moving, and make easy targets for hunters, and both may soon join their giant relative, becoming nothing more than a memory.

▽ Manatees are distant relatives of elephants.

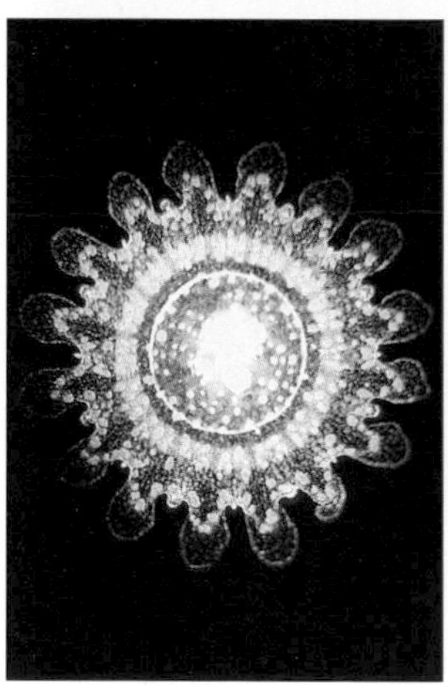

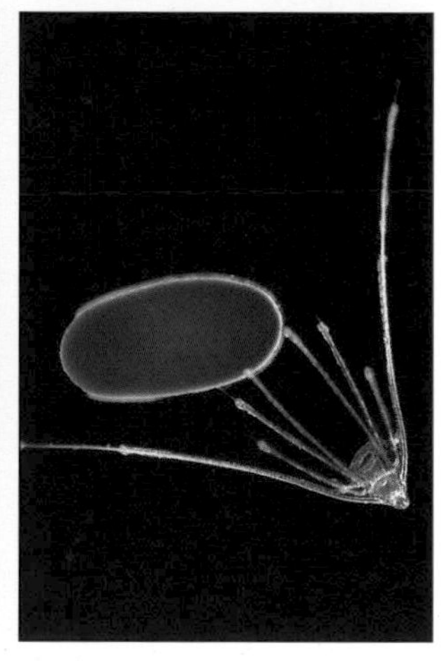

△ The roots of mangroves show up clearly at low tide. The trees may be cut (inset) for firewood.

◁ The larvae of jellyfish (left), sponges, and brittlestars (right) are among the tiny animals that shelter in mangrove swamps.

Marvelous mangroves

Around the edges of the tropical oceans, huge areas of coastline are covered with dense, muddy **mangrove** swamps. These swamps form the basis of a food web that sustains a rich variety of animals.

Dead leaves from the trees are constantly falling into the swamps, where they slowly break down into small particles. These leaf particles provide an endless feast for hundreds of different animals—shellfish, shrimps, crabs, marine worms, and fish.

Some of these animals stay in the mangroves, but many others migrate in from the sea as newly hatched larvae (the young form of some animals). The tangled roots of the mangroves provide shelter for these youngsters, and there are far fewer predators here than there are out at sea. As they mature, the larvae leave the mangrove nursery and migrate back to the deeper waters, where they become part of other food chains. The wind and tides also carry large quantities of leaf particles out to sea, where they feed other marine communities.

The mangrove swamp, either directly or indirectly, feeds many of the fish in tropical waters. The ecosystem also sustains millions of human beings who depend on local catches of fish as a source of protein. Research has shown that, with proper management, a mangrove swamp can produce as much protein as the same area of agricultural land.

Shrinking resources

Each year, thousands of acres of mangrove are cut down for firewood and thousands more are cleared for housing development. The trees are also cut to provide wood chips for papermaking. Some countries have already lost up to 40 percent of their mangroves in this way.

When an area of mangrove swamp is lost, the food web is cut at the base. The loss of this marine nursery can have far-reaching effects on other coastal ecosystems, and there is a noticeable decline in fish populations extending far out to sea. In Australia, however, the government has recognized the value of mangroves to offshore fishing grounds and has banned any development or commercial exploitation of the mangroves along the country's northern coast.

▽ Giant clams have been collected for food, but now they are becoming rare.

Beyond the mangroves

The giant clam, over three feet long and weighing over 500 pounds, is more than a match for any farm animal found on dry land. Giant clams are able to grow to this astonishing size because they can make their own food from sunlight. Giant clams live in the shallow waters around coral reefs, and like the corals, giant clams have single-celled algae in their bodies (see page 26).

The flesh of the giant clam tastes delicious, but wild clams have now become a rare delicacy. So many have been collected for food in some parts of the world that the giant clam has disappeared completely.

In order to reestablish the giant clam, scientists have learned how to hatch and grow baby clams in tanks. When the young clams are big enough to survive in the wild, they can be "planted out" on a reef.

This same technique could be used to farm the clams on a large scale. Although raising and planting the young clams is a fairly expensive and time-consuming business, that is all there is to do. Giant clams require nothing but sunlight and clean water in order to grow, and the sheer size of each harvest makes the initial effort worthwhile.

tropical—found between the tropics of cancer and capricorn.
subtropical—found between the tropical and temperate lands.
polyps—individual animals that live in colonies. The polyp has a hollow body with a ring of tentacles around the mouth.
parasite—any organism that lives on or in another plant or animal and takes food from its body.
erosion—the wearing away of sand, soil, or rock by water, wind, etc.
reptile—any of the group of cold-blooded vertebrates that includes turtles, snakes, and crocodiles.
mangrove—any of the tropical trees with stiltlike roots that grow in salt water by the coast.

Temperate coastlines

△ On some beaches, drains and sewers empty waste directly into the sea.

▷ Factories on the banks of the Seine in France pour waste materials into the river, which carries them out into the sea.

Home waters

Most (86 percent) marine pollution comes from factories and farms. Although the pollution eventually spreads out in the great oceans, it tends to become concentrated in coastal waters. The problem is most severe in developed countries where heavy industry and intensive agriculture greatly increase the amount of pollution flowing into the sea. Many areas of water around Europe and North America are now very polluted.

Under natural conditions, marine life flourishes in river estuaries. Sadly, this is often no longer true. In Europe, for example, the Rhine alone carries 300,000 tons of waste into the North Sea each year. The most immediate effect is that estuaries develop very high levels of pollution. Activities such as fishing and raising shellfish, which were once found in most estuaries, are becoming rare.

Clean beaches and safe swimming

People like going to the seaside, and whether they swim, surf, or just splash about, they expect the sea to be a clean and safe environment. However, in some places there is now a small but definite risk of catching diseases from seawater. This problem has occurred because many countries continue to pump raw sewage directly into the sea.

Until recently, it was widely believed that the sea could absorb any amount of raw sewage without lasting harm. But studies have shown that there is now too much waste for the sea to deal with. Some of the microorganisms in sewage that cause disease are able to survive up to 17 months in seawater. In many areas, swimmers run the risk of sore throats, itching eyes, and upset stomachs. The only solution is to ensure that all sewage is treated and disinfected before it enters the sea.

The situation is particularly bad in Britain, where in 1988, one-third of the officially recognized swimming beaches failed to meet health standards established by the European Community. The government has since launched a $4 billion cleanup program, and the position is slowly improving.

Natural poisons?

In many cases of marine pollution, the link between cause and effect is not always obvious. One of the most poisonous substances in the sea is a natural toxin (poison) produced by certain species of single-celled algae. Sometimes the toxin-producing species form great blooms.

The toxin builds up in animal bodies through the process of bioconcentration (see page 9), and shellfish that feed by filtering seawater are the first to be affected. Every year, a number of people are poisoned, quite accidentally, by eating seafood that contains toxin.

Although toxic blooms can occur naturally, they are known to be encouraged

by the nutrients in sewage and fertilizer. Many people suspect that some recent outbreaks may have more to do with pollution than with natural causes.

The shore, wet and dry

The seashore forms a special kind of marine environment, one that is halfway between land and water. The plants and animals that live on the shore have adapted to changing conditions of wet and dry caused by the daily rise and fall of the tides. In some regions—around the Mediterranean, for example—the difference between high and low tides is only a few feet. In other areas, however, the tide rises and falls by as much as 30 feet.

The shore is an excellent place to study some of the basic principles of marine ecosystems.

Rocky shores

Zonation is a feature of all marine environments. At sea, and on the seashore, plants and animals tend to live in distinct zones. At sea, the zones form at different depths, depending on how much light is available for photosynthesis. On the seashore, the most important factor in zonation is the amount of time that marine life is uncovered by the tide and exposed to the drying effects of the air.

Rocky shorelines show the clearest evidence of zonation, and always follow the same basic pattern. Farthest from the sea, in the splash zone, are found black lichens that can tolerate salt water. Below the lichens is a zone containing wrack seaweeds, and around the low water mark this blends into the zone containing oarweed and kelp. The plant life in the two lower zones provides food and living space for many marine animals. One square yard of knotted wrack may contain as many as 200,000 animals, most of them very tiny. Larger animals include shellfish such as mussels, barnacles, limpets, and whelks, and several species of crab.

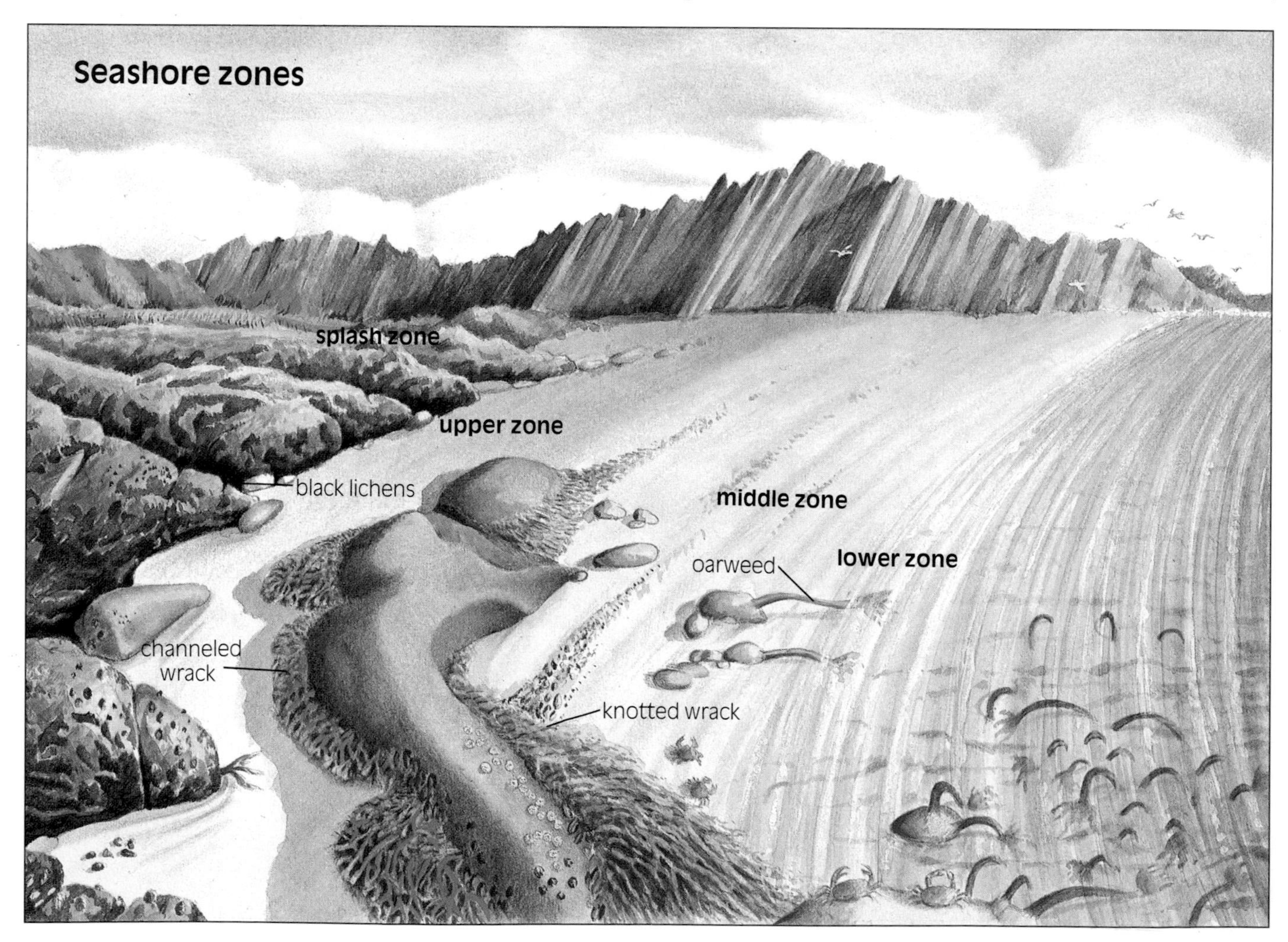

Sandy shores
On sandy shores, marine life is much scarcer, because the sand provides no firm footholds. Those animals that do live on sandy shores survive by burrowing into the sand when the tide is out. Most of them emerge to feed when the tide comes in, but others remain buried under the sand.

The peacock worm is a filter feeder that extends feathery fronds under water to capture food particles. The tellin, a type of shellfish, feeds by "vacuuming" the surface of the sand through a siphon (long tube) that is pushed up from the shell. Animals that are more mobile, such as the masked crab, use the sand only as a temporary shelter, and when the tide is in they come out to scavenge and hunt. While it is buried under the sand, the masked crab breathes through its long pointed "beak."

Watch out!

Ecology watchers must be constantly on the alert for new forms of pollution.

Some of the plants and animals that cling to rocky shores are equally happy growing on the underside of boats. Antifouling paint is used to stop this marine growth, which makes boats much slower in the water.

This paint works by slowly releasing tiny quantities of poisonous chemicals known as TBTs, which prevent life from growing on anything covered with it. Reports from Canada, Britain, Singapore, France, and Japan all suggest that the level of TBTs in seawater is having harmful effects on more than 40 marine species. For example, TBTs cause oysters to grow thicker shells, which means less meat. The dangers of TBTs are now well recognized and many countries have introduced controls on the use of antifouling paint, but none has yet banned it completely.

△ Often, the only way to clean up after an oil spill is by hand.

A coating of oil

Millions of tons of oil are transported across the oceans each year in giant supertankers. However, oil is also one of the most dangerous forms of marine pollution. There have been several big accidents in coastal waters, which have caused considerable damage to local ecosystems. Oil floats on water, and when it leaks from a damaged tanker it forms large slicks that may cover many square miles. If an oil slick is carried ashore by the wind and the tide, it can cover whole stretches of coastline, smothering and poisoning all forms of marine life.

Cleaning up after an oil spill is a very difficult and expensive business. During the first incidents, governments tried to disperse the oil by spraying it with large quantities of detergent. They succeeded in moving most of the oil, but the detergent proved to be even more poisonous to marine life than the oil and this method has now been abandoned. In some cases, the only safe solution is to laboriously gather the oil from rocks and beaches and carry it away in trucks. More modern techniques try to skim the oil from the surface of the sea before it reaches the coast, but it takes time to get the special equipment in place, and by then it may be too late to save the beach.

A lost cause

Seabirds are particularly at risk because the oil clogs their feathers, and even small quantities can prevent flight. Birds try to clean the oil off by preening with their beaks, but usually succeed only in swallowing enough oil to be poisoned. Those that are totally covered with oil are almost certain to die, even if they are rescued and cleaned by human volunteers.

Some seabirds are vulnerable to oil pollution out at sea. Those that dive for their food often mistake an oil slick for a shoal of fish, and swoop down, only to become stuck in the oil. Somes species, such as puffins, guillemots, and razorbills, gather in huge floating "rafts" before the breeding season. If an oil slick drifts into such a raft, many thousands of birds may be affected.

Seabirds are also threatened by other types of marine pollution. Most seabirds are at the top of the ocean's food web, and therefore receive maximum doses of pollution through the process of bioconcentration. In many areas the level of DDT in some seabirds is more than 10,000 times the level found in seawater. One effect of DDT in birds is to make the eggshells thinner, which means that more eggs get

▷ This albatross colony is on the Falkland Islands.

▽ Oil can be removed from these penguins using a chemical solution. More often, birds are too heavily coated with oil (inset) to be saved.

broken, and fewer chicks hatch. As a result, the population gets smaller and smaller. In the United States, the brown pelican was nearly wiped out before DDT was banned, although its numbers are increasing again.

Dying for fashion

The albatross is the largest of all seabirds, with a wingspan of up to 11½ feet. For most of the year, they live ranging across thousands of miles of ocean. Only at their traditional breeding colonies, often on remote islands, are they ever found in any numbers.

During the last century, there was a worldwide fashion for feathers, especially albatross feathers because they were the largest. Many of the more accessible albatross colonies were repeatedly raided by greedy hunters. Some populations have never recovered properly, and the Amsterdam and short-tailed albatross are now seriously endangered.

Back from the brink

One of the rarest of all seabirds is the cahow, a species of petrel found only on the island of Bermuda. During the eighteenth century, settlers slaughtered thousands of cahows for food, and for many years they were thought to have become extinct.

In 1951, the first living cahows to be seen for nearly 300 years were found nesting on a small offshore island. In total, there were just 14 birds, and every effort was made to protect them.

When protecting a bird species, the safety of the eggs is the most important factor, and other animals usually present the greatest threat. The cahows' eggs had to be protected from rats that stole them for food, and from other birds that tried to take over the cahows' nests. Today, after 40 years of protection, there are about 100 cahows, and the species now has a fair chance of survival.

Seals and sea otters

Ecology watching is like being a detective. There may be plenty of clues, but it is not always easy to prove that, for example, pollution is a killer.

During the spring of 1988, seals began dying off the coast of Denmark and Sweden, and within weeks, hundreds of dead seals had been washed ashore. By August, dead seals were being found in all the countries surrounding the North and Baltic seas.

At first, scientists were baffled. They suspected that pollution was causing the deaths, but tests showed that the seals were dying from a little-known disease called phocine distemper.

This disease, which is caused by a virus, is rare among wild seals, and does not normally cause mass deaths. Most scientists became convinced that some other factor must be invovled.

Throughout the summer, seals died by the thousands, with more than 2,000 dead in Britain alone. As winter approached, the disease seemed to fade away, but it reappeared in 1989, causing many deaths among newly born seal pups. Scientists continued to study the problem, and some seals were even fitted with miniature radio transmitters so that they could be tracked to find the mystery source of the disease, but without success.

Continuing research has eventually shown that infected seals have high levels of PCBs (see page 17) in their bodies. Although it has not yet been proved, it seems almost certain that PCBs are somehow lowering the seals' natural resistance to phocine distemper.

There is no longer any mystery about the death of the seals, and the killer has been identified. But that does not solve the problem; the pollution remains in the sea, threatening all forms of marine life.

A common seal pup suffering from phocine distemper

Hidden problems of protection

Most people agree that endangered species should be protected. But this is not always as simple as it seems. Life exists as a balance. Sometimes, however, protecting a species also causes upset. A good example of this is the case of the California sea otter.

Once hunted for its fur, the California sea otter was thought to have become extinct. During the 1930s a small group of survivors was discovered and has been protected ever since. Today there are about 1,700 sea otters living off the coast of California.

△ Giant kelp thrives where sea otters control the populations of sea urchins. But sea otters also eat clams (right), collected by shellfish farmers.

Sea otters feed mainly on sea urchins and clams. When there were only a few otters, these invertebrates flourished and a sizable shellfish industry was established in the waters off California. However, sea urchins feed on giant kelp (a large brown seaweed) and kelp farmers consider sea urchins to be a major pest.

As the number of sea otters have increased, the kelp farmers have found that they have far fewer problems with the sea urchins. However, the people who depend on shellfish for a living are now complaining because the sea otters are eating most of the clams. Put very simply:

—More otters means fewer sea urchins, which means more kelp.

—Fewer otters means more clams, but less kelp.

In California, people still argue about whether sea otters should be considered a pest or a protected species. In these circumstances, it is very hard to say who is right and who is wrong, but for the meantime at least, the sea otters remain safe.

The future

Farming the oceans

The three Ps—Preserving the natural environment, Preventing further pollution, and Protecting endangered species—are a way of making up for our past mistakes. But these form only a part of our responsibilities toward the earth's seas and oceans. Probably the most important factor in the future health of the sea is its position in the human food web. If the sea is going to continue to play a major role in feeding the world, we have got to stop behaving like hunter-gatherers, and instead become true farmers of the sea.

Farming the sea is not a new idea, and small-scale mariculture has been practiced for centuries. Oysters and other shellfish are raised all over the world. Farming fish, however, presents more of a problem. The main difficulty is that, unlike land, the sea does not divide easily into large fields, and at present, fish farming is restricted to much smaller enclosures.

Recently, intensive mariculture has become big business in many large countries. Fish such as salmon are raised in a series of floating cages anchored in shallow water. A farm may contain as many as half a million fish. Concentrating so many fish within a very limited area is already leading to pollution problems.

In some areas, leftover food and waste products from the fish are building up on the seabed. These additional nutrients are upsetting the balance of the food web in local ecosystems. The situation is made worse by the fact that fish kept in crowded conditions are especially prone to parasites. Farmers have to use large quantities of pesticide to keep their fish free of sea lice, and these powerful chemicals are leaking into the marine environment.

Caged in

The obvious answer is to give the fish more room, but there are limits to the size of cage that can be built. The constant motion of tides and currents means that large structures are constantly being pulled and pushed out of shape and position. Lightweight nets cannot be used, because a net that will safely enclose a farmed species is likely to be a lethal trap for many wild species. Success in ocean farming depends on adopting entirely new approaches, and it may be possible to learn from the whales.

△ Humpback whales feed inside a circle of bubbles.

A barrier of bubbles

Humpback whales sometimes gather and trap shoals of krill in circular nets of bubbles up to 100 feet across. One or two whales will swim below the shoal, then spiral upward with bubbles streaming from their blowholes. At the surface, the bubbles form a barrier that seems to prevent the krill from escaping while the whales feed. It may be possible for us to apply similar techniques in shallow waters. A network of air pipes on the seabed could be used to form walls of bubbles, behind which shoals of food fish could be raised.

Extensive mariculture (farming the open seas without enclosures) is also a possibility, but again there are problems. More than 50 years ago, several European governments experimented with raising young flatfish in tanks, releasing them into the sea, then trawling them up again after they had grown to adult size.

In one sense, the experiments were a success. The fish raised in captivity grew much faster and larger than wild fish. Unfortunately, the governments could not agree who owned which fish. Marking each fish before it's release was not really practical. Lack of international agreement soon caused the project to be abandoned.

Plant life

An alternative method of taking food from the sea may be to cultivate seaweed on a large scale. In several countries, local inhabitants already collect small quantities of seaweed for food. In California, giant kelp is harvested commercially. Giant kelp is the largest of the seaweeds and under the right conditions can grow to more than 200 feet in length. At present, most of the harvest is processed to provide thickening agents for the food industry. However, kelp can also be processed to produce methane (a valuable fuel) and the residue used as animal feed or fertilizer.

One of the main problems with kelp farming is that, like all large seaweeds, kelp only grows in shallow coastal waters, where it can anchor itself to the seabed. These coastal waters are already the most polluted and the most crowded. One scientist has proposed that we move the giant kelp out to sea by constructing large mid - ocean farms. A network of underwater lines about 130 feet below the surface, covering several square miles, would provide anchorage for the kelp. In addition, shellfish could be raised, and the presence of the kelp would probably cause fish populations to increase.

▽ Dolphins could help us to farm the seas.

Talk to the animals

If we are ever going to farm the open range of the wild sea, we are going to need help. Despite all our technical advances we are still slow and clumsy underwater compared with fish. Dolphins, however, are superbly adapted to life in the sea. They are also quick learners, and can be trained to obey whistled commands in the same way as sheepdogs. Dolphins are the obvious candidates to be our helpers in the sea.

Experiments have shown that dolphins can learn and remember simple languages, but not human speech. Two types of language have been used—hand signals, and computer sounds played through underwater loudspeakers. Although progress is slow, scientists have already shown that dolphins can understand "sentences" of up to five "words," and can carry out simple tasks, such as searching for an object and showing where it is. Given time, it seems entirely possible that dolphins could become our sheepdogs of the sea.

Global solutions

Declining fish populations is a very complex problem, and it is very tempting to look for simple solutions. But there is much that we don't understand, and we should therefore proceed with caution.

Some recent studies have shown that phytoplankton growth is stimulated by increased quantities of iron in seawater. Some scientists have suggested sprinkling thousands of tons of iron particles into the sea so that more phytoplankton will grow. This would provide more food for animals higher up the food chain and eventually more food for humans.

But this may be a dangerous course of action, because we still know far too little about phytoplankton. There is a risk that seeding the seas with iron could cause eutrophication on a massive scale, leaving huge areas completely lifeless.

▽ Strange tubelike animals and new species of crab (inset) have been discovered around volcanic vents on the sea bed.

New ecologies

Research is our most important tool in learning how to live in harmony with the seas and oceans. Not all research provides results that are immediately useful. Sometimes, research just serves to show us that the oceans are still full of surprises.

In 1977, deep-sea explorers found a whole new ecology of life clustered around underwater volcanic vents more than 8,000 feet below the surface. Some of the species that were discovered work in a completely different way from the rest of life on earth. They have no mouths or digestive systems, and exist by absorbing the minerals and chemicals that flow out of the volcanic vents. Other species, such as crabs, are more familiar, but all of them are adapted to life at great depths and cannot survive at the surface.

At present we can only gaze in wonder at these incredible deep-sea communities, but at some time in the future, we may be able to put this new knowledge to good use.